Crafts for
Valentine's Day

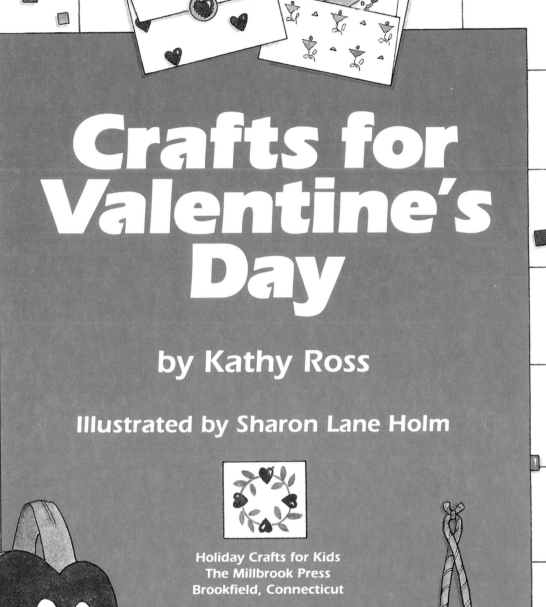

Crafts for Valentine's Day

by Kathy Ross

Illustrated by Sharon Lane Holm

Holiday Crafts for Kids
The Millbrook Press
Brookfield, Connecticut

To Greyson and Allison—K.R.

To Michael—S.H.L.

Library of Congress Cataloging-in-Publication Data
Ross, Kathy (Katharine Reynolds), 1948-
Crafts for Valentine's Day/by Kathy Ross;
illustrated by Sharon Lane Holm.
p. cm. — (Holiday Crafts for Kids)
Presents 20 simple Valentine's Day related crafts that
young children can make from everyday material.
ISBN 1-56294-489-4 (lib.bdg.) ISBN 1-56294-887-3 (pbk.)
1. Valentine decorations—Juvenile literature.
2. Handicraft—Juvenile literature. [1. Valentine
decorations. 2. Handicraft.] I. Holm, Sharon
Lane, ill. II. Title. III. Series.
TT900.V34R68 1995
745.594'1—dc20 94-9834 CIP AC

Published by The Millbrook Press
2 Old New Milford Road
Brookfield, Connecticut 06804

Contents

Happy Valentine's Day!

Valentine's Day is celebrated on February 14. It is a time for telling family and friends—and sometimes someone you wish you were friends with—how much you care about them. People do this by sending valentines—paper cards and hearts with a valentine message written on them.

No one is really sure how Valentine's Day actually got started. Some believe it originated with a priest named Valentine who lived a long time ago. It is believed that he secretly married young lovers who had been forbidden to marry by the laws of the time. Another story tells of a man named Valentine who was sent to prison for his religious beliefs. It is said that the children of his town loved him very much and sent notes and flowers to him in prison.

Today we celebrate Valentine's Day by exchanging cards, candy, and flowers. It is not a legal holiday on which schools, banks, and post offices are closed, but it is just the right time for telling people you care about them.

Wallpaper Envelopes

Make your valentine mail extra special by sending paper hearts in these beautiful envelopes.

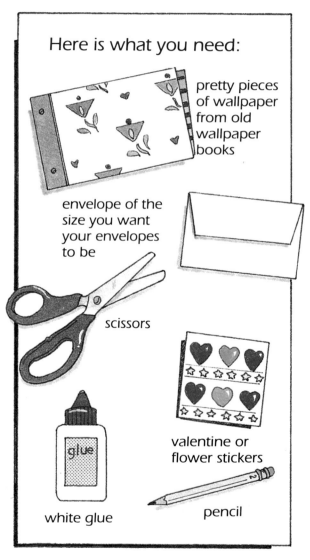

Here is what you need:

pretty pieces of wallpaper from old wallpaper books

envelope of the size you want your envelopes to be

scissors

valentine or flower stickers

white glue

pencil

Here is what you do:

1. Carefully unglue the seams of your envelope and flatten it out to use as a pattern. Steam helps to loosen the glue, so leaving the envelope in the bathroom while you shower should make it come apart quite easily.

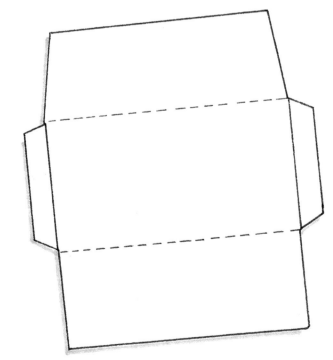

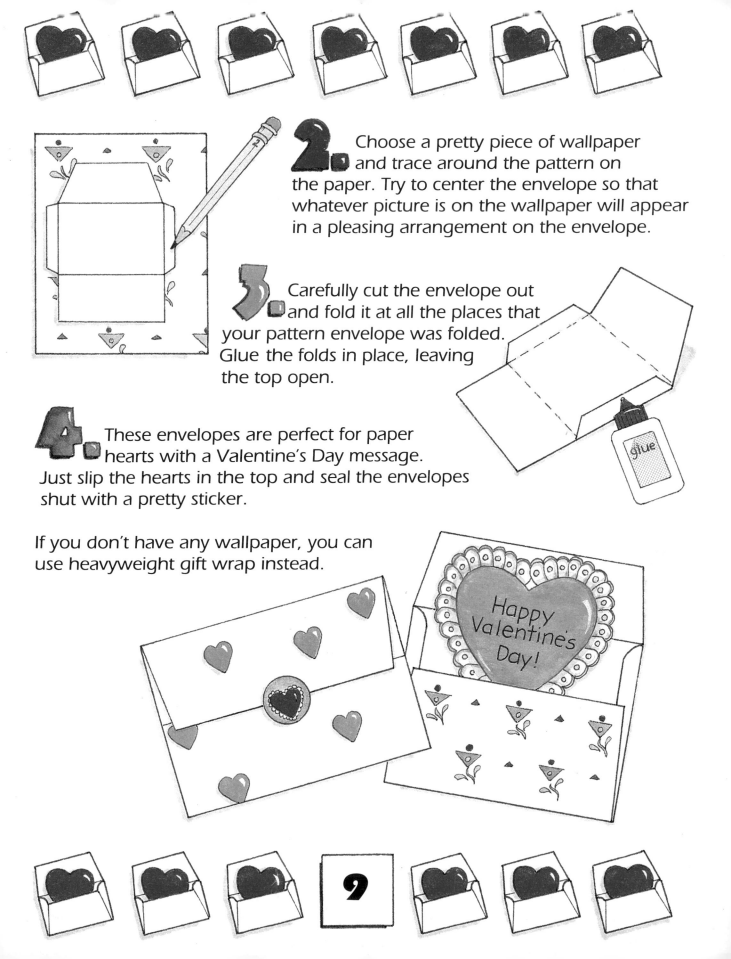

2. Choose a pretty piece of wallpaper and trace around the pattern on the paper. Try to center the envelope so that whatever picture is on the wallpaper will appear in a pleasing arrangement on the envelope.

3. Carefully cut the envelope out and fold it at all the places that your pattern envelope was folded. Glue the folds in place, leaving the top open.

4. These envelopes are perfect for paper hearts with a Valentine's Day message. Just slip the hearts in the top and seal the envelopes shut with a pretty sticker.

If you don't have any wallpaper, you can use heavyweight gift wrap instead.

Happy Valentine's Day!

Heart Mouse

Whoever gets to pull on the tail of this little heart mouse will get a surprise.

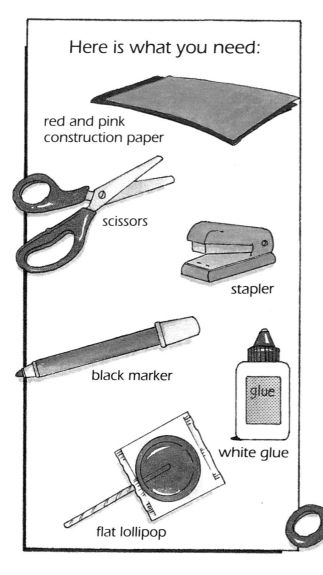

Here is what you need:

red and pink construction paper

scissors

stapler

black marker

white glue

flat lollipop

Here is what you do:

1. Fold a piece of red construction paper and cut a half heart about 3 1/2 inches (9 centimeters) high on the fold. Leave the heart folded to form the body of the mouse.

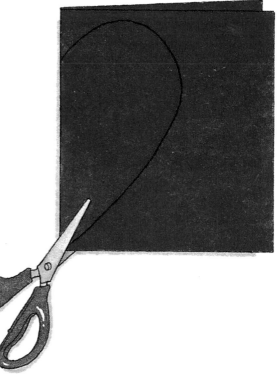

10

2. Cut a smaller heart from the red paper for the head of the mouse. Cut a slit about halfway up from the point of the heart. Wrap the two sides of the slit around to form a cone nose and staple them in place. Use a black marker to draw eyes and a nose. Staple the head to the pointed end of the heart body. Staple the rounded end of the body so that it forms a pocket.

3. Cut a tiny heart from red paper. Write PULL on the heart and glue it to the stick end of the lollipop. Cut a heart from pink paper to cover the lollipop. Write your valentine message on this heart and glue it over the wrapper. Tuck the lollipop into the body of the mouse so that the stick end is sticking out to form the tail of the mouse.

Make a mouse for each of your friends.

Valentine Puppet

Here is what you need:

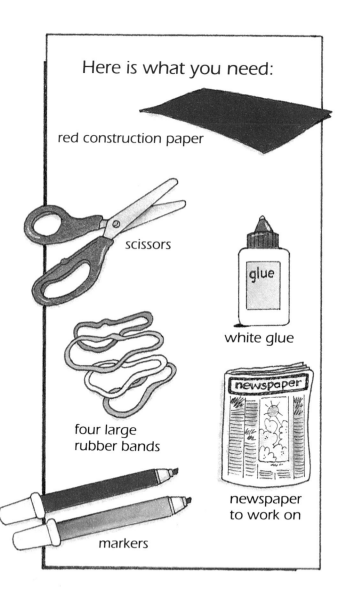

red construction paper

scissors

white glue

four large
rubber bands

newspaper
to work on

markers

Here is what you do:

1. Cut two hearts of the same size from red construction paper. Make them bigger than your hand. Cut four 1-inch (2.5-centimeter) hearts from the red paper for the puppet's hands and feet.

12

2. Cut each of the rubber bands so that they form long elastic strings. Glue the rubber bands to the sides and bottom of one of the large hearts to form the arms and the legs of the puppet.

3. Glue the tops of the two large hearts together with the ends of the rubber bands between them. Leave the bottom part open to slip your hand in.

4. Glue a small heart to the end of each elastic arm and leg.

5. When the puppet has dried completely, draw on a face with markers.

This happy heart puppet loves to swing its arms and legs around.

13

Valentine Crown

Make a friend feel like royalty with this crown.

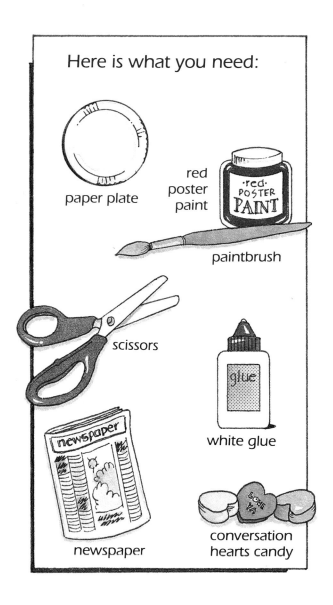

Here is what you need:

paper plate

red poster paint

paintbrush

scissors

white glue

newspaper

conversation hearts candy

Here is what you do:

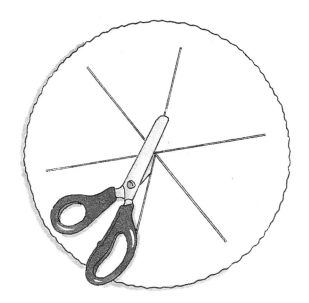

1. Cut a slit across the middle of the plate, starting about 1 inch (2.5 centimeters) inside the outer rim and stopping about an inch inside the rim on the opposite side of the plate. Starting in the center of the plate, cut four more slits to create six pie-shaped sections. Fold the sections up to make a crown.

2. Paint the plate red on both sides and let it dry.

RED POSTER PAINT

3. Decorate the crown by gluing conversation hearts on each point.

Crown someone the king or queen of your heart.

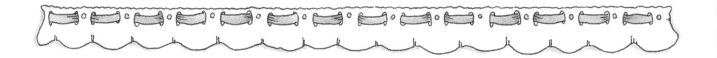

Heart Dove Hat

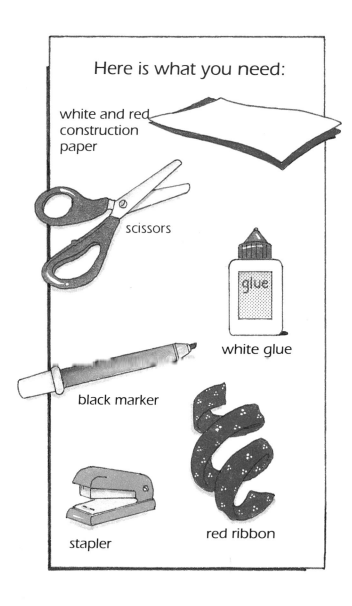

Here is what you need:

white and red construction paper

scissors

white glue

black marker

stapler

red ribbon

Here is what you do:

1. Fold a 12- by 18-inch (30- by 45-centimeter) piece of white construction paper in half and cut a 7-inch (18-centimeter) heart on the fold. This will be the body of the dove. Fold a second piece of construction paper and cut a 5-inch (13-centimeter) heart on the fold for the wings. Cut a 4-inch (10-centimeter) heart on the fold for the head.

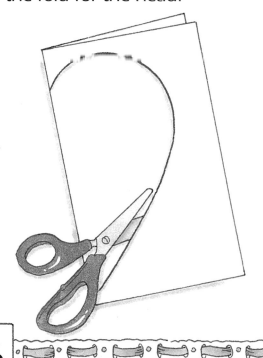

2. Glue the small heart over the folded point of the large heart so that the point of the small heart sticks out to form the beak. Glue the rounded end of the medium heart over the back of the bird to form wings.

3. Cut a red heart for the dove to carry in its beak. Write a valentine message on both sides of the heart with black marker. Cut a small slit in the beak and glue the red heart in place. Use the black marker to draw eyes on the dove.

4. Staple a long piece of red ribbon to each side of the dove so that you can tie the bird to your head as a pretty valentine hat.

Tying this dove to your head will also keep it from flying away!

Card Man Favors

Here is what you need:

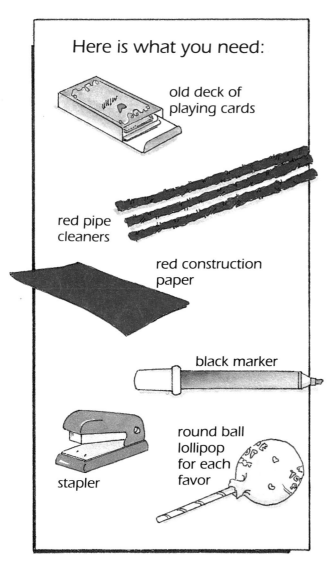

old deck of playing cards

red pipe cleaners

red construction paper

black marker

stapler

round ball lollipop for each favor

Here is what you do:

1. For each favor you will need a heart playing card for the front and an extra card to use as the back. Only the back of this card will show.

2. Cut arms and legs from red pipe cleaners. Hold them in place by stapling them between the two playing cards.

3. Cut a heart-shaped head from red paper and draw on a face with a black marker. Staple the head to the top of the card man. Cut a smaller heart and write the name of the friend you are giving the favor to on the heart. Poke it onto one of the pipe cleaner hands.

4. Wrap the other arm around a lollipop. Bend the bottom of the pipe cleaner legs to form feet.

With a little bending and arranging of the legs, these figures will stand up if you wish to use them as table favors at a party.

Valentine Mail Vest

This vest has a pocket for collecting all your valentine mail.

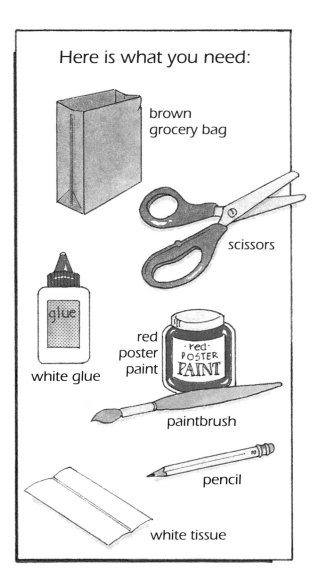

Here is what you need:

brown grocery bag

scissors

white glue

red poster paint

paintbrush

pencil

white tissue

Here is what you do:

1. Cut the bag along the seam. Then cut the bottom out so that you have a long strip of brown paper. Fold the strip in half and cut a neck hole at the fold and a 4-inch (10-centimeter) slit down the back. The bag should now fit over your head like a vest, with half the bag in front of you and half in back of you.

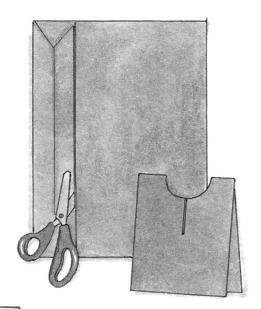

2. Fold the two front, bottom corners of the bag up and in to form the bottom point of a heart. Glue them together. This will form the pocket for your valentine mail. Sketch the top part of the heart on the vest. Then paint the entire heart red.

3. When the paint has dried, outline the heart with white glue and stick bits of shredded tissue around it to look like lace.

You can use the glue and shredded tissue to write your name on the front of the heart if you wish.

Castle Mail Holder

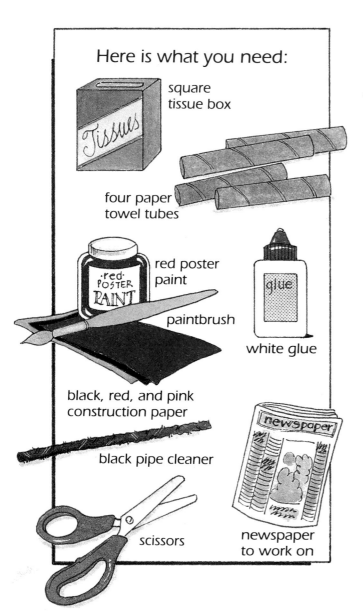

Here is what you need:

square tissue box

four paper towel tubes

red poster paint

paintbrush

white glue

black, red, and pink construction paper

black pipe cleaner

scissors

newspaper to work on

Here is what you do:

1. Trim the four paper towel tubes so that they are 3 inches (8 centimeters) taller than the tissue box. Cut eight evenly spaced, 1-inch (2.5-centimeter) slits around the top of each tube. Fold in every other tab around each tube to form the castle turrets.

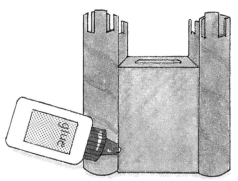

2. Glue a tube on each corner of the box to make the castle. After the glue has dried, paint the castle red.

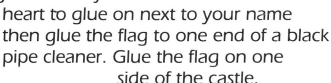

3. Cut a door and windows for the castle from black paper and glue them on. Cut hearts from red and pink paper to decorate the castle. Cut a pink triangle flag and write your name on it. Cut a red heart to glue on next to your name then glue the flag to one end of a black pipe cleaner. Glue the flag on one side of the castle.

Keep this castle mail holder on your desk all year to stash your special notes and letters in.

Happy Heart Mailbag

If you are expecting lots and lots of valentines, this happy heart mailbag is the one for you.

Here is what you need:

brown grocery bag

scissors

red, black, white, and pink construction paper

black marker

white glue

Here is what you do:

1. From red construction paper, cut a heart as wide as the bag and about two thirds as tall as the bag. Glue the heart to the front of the bag. Trim the top of the bag off around the top of the heart.

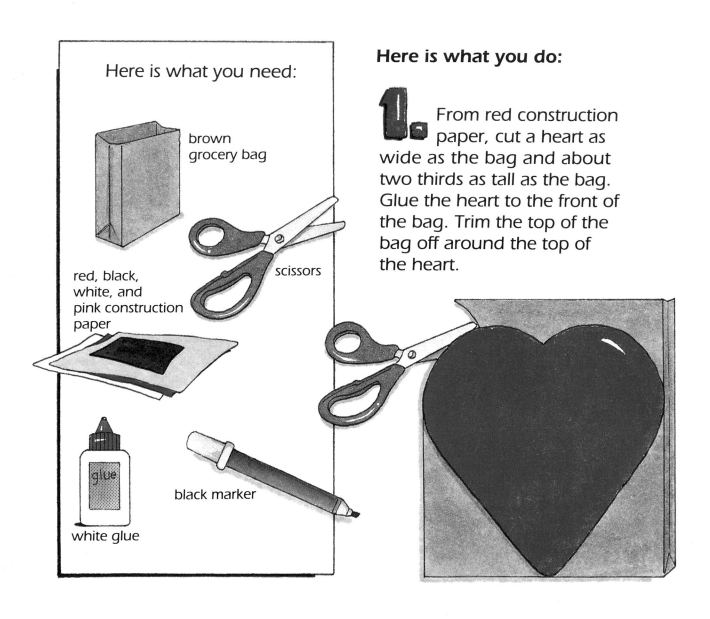

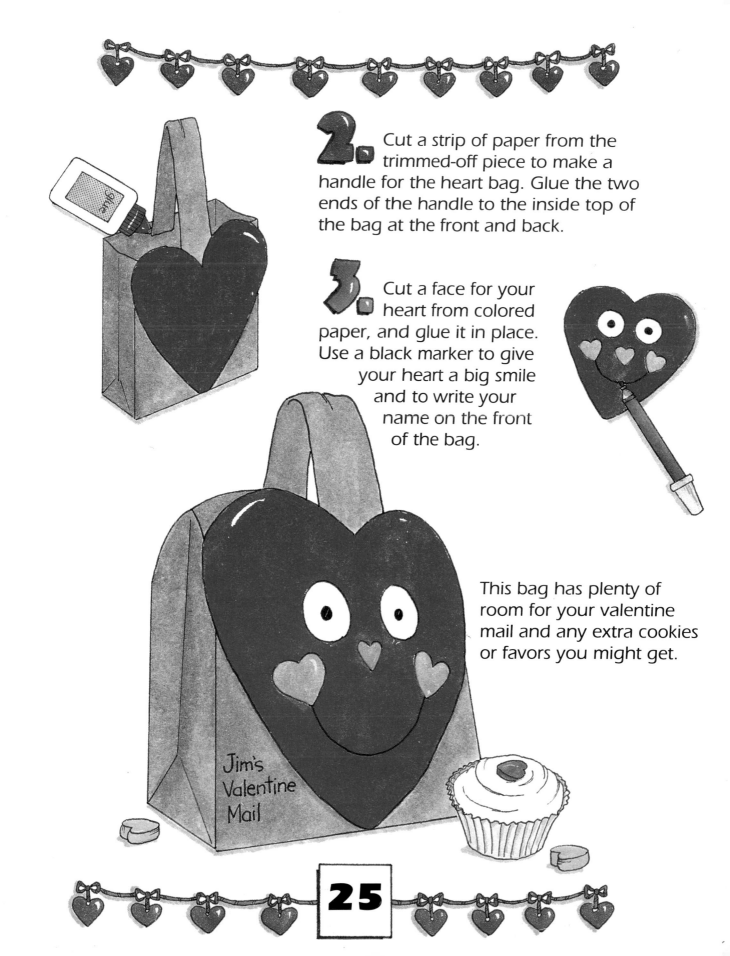

2. Cut a strip of paper from the trimmed-off piece to make a handle for the heart bag. Glue the two ends of the handle to the inside top of the bag at the front and back.

3. Cut a face for your heart from colored paper, and glue it in place. Use a black marker to give your heart a big smile and to write your name on the front of the bag.

This bag has plenty of room for your valentine mail and any extra cookies or favors you might get.

Jim's Valentine Mail

Dove Table Decoration

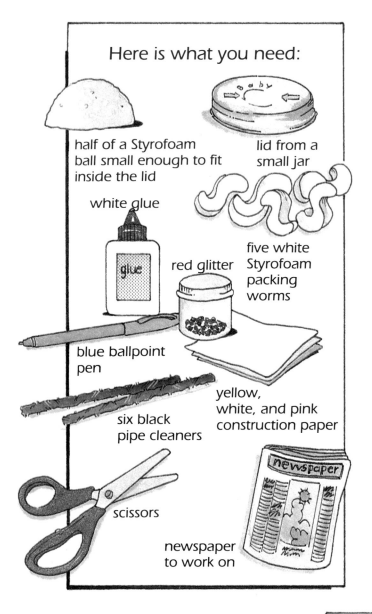

Here is what you need:

half of a Styrofoam ball small enough to fit inside the lid

lid from a small jar

white glue

red glitter

five white Styrofoam packing worms

blue ballpoint pen

six black pipe cleaners

yellow, white, and pink construction paper

scissors

newspaper to work on

Here is what you do:

1. Glue the flat side of the half Styrofoam ball into the jar lid. Cover the sides of the jar lid and the ball with white glue and sprinkle with red glitter to completely cover.

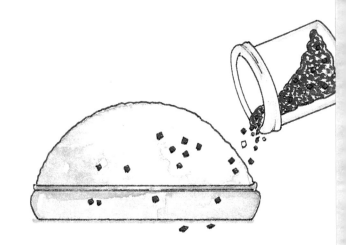

2. Stick one packing worm on the end of each pipe cleaner and poke the other ends into the Styrofoam ball.

3. To make each dove, cut wings and a tail feather from white paper and a beak from yellow paper. Glue them in place on each dove. Cut tiny hearts from pink paper to glue in each bird's mouth. Add eyes with a ballpoint pen.

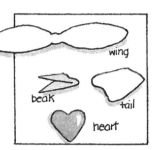

wing

beak

tail

heart

These valentine doves will look very sweet flying around on the table of someone special to you.

Hearts and Flowers Wreath

Here is what you need:

eggs

two cardboard egg cartons

paper plate

scissors

Styrofoam trays

red, purple, and green poster paint

·red· POSTER PAINT

·Purple· POSTER PAINT

·Green· POSTER PAINT

paintbrush

newspaper

yellow tissue

glue

green yarn

newspaper to work on

Here is what you do:

1. Cut eight cups from an egg carton. Cut four slits around each cup to make them look like flowers. Cut sixteen leaves from the tops of the egg cartons. If you cut some of them from the bend in the top, they will have a nice curved look. Cut eight hearts from the tops. Cut some of these on the bend, too, so that they are not all flat.

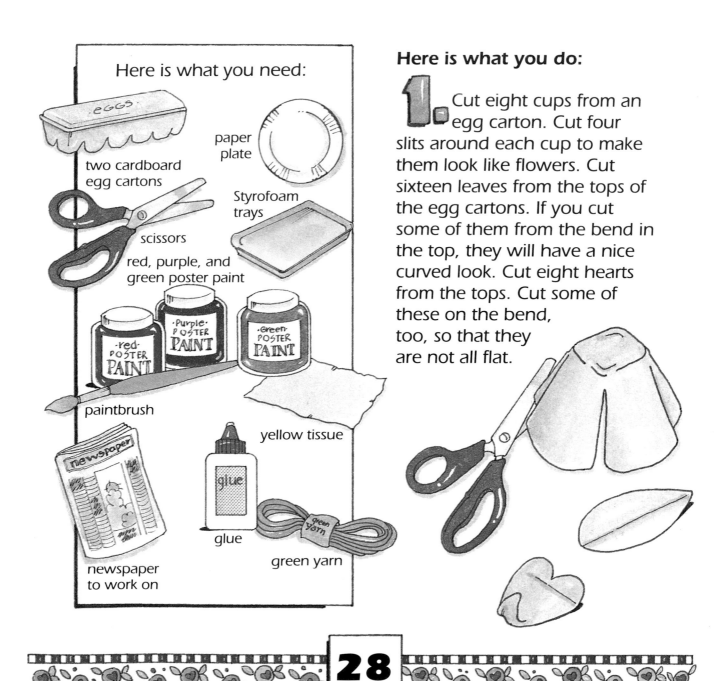

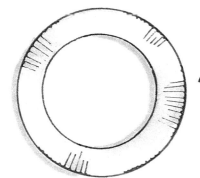

2. Cut the center out of a paper plate to make a wreath frame. Paint the wreath green. Paint the leaves green, the flowers purple, and the hearts red. Put everything on Styrofoam trays to dry.

3. Tie a piece of green yarn to the top of the wreath, to make a hanger. Spread glue on the frame and arrange the flowers around the wreath, with two leaves under each flower and a heart in between each flower. Crumple a small piece of yellow tissue to glue in the center of each flower.

4. When the wreath is completely dry, hang it on your front door for Valentine's Day.

This beautiful wreath is worth the time it takes to make.

Valentine Card Garland

Here is a great way to use old valentines and decorate your room at the same time.

Here is what you need:

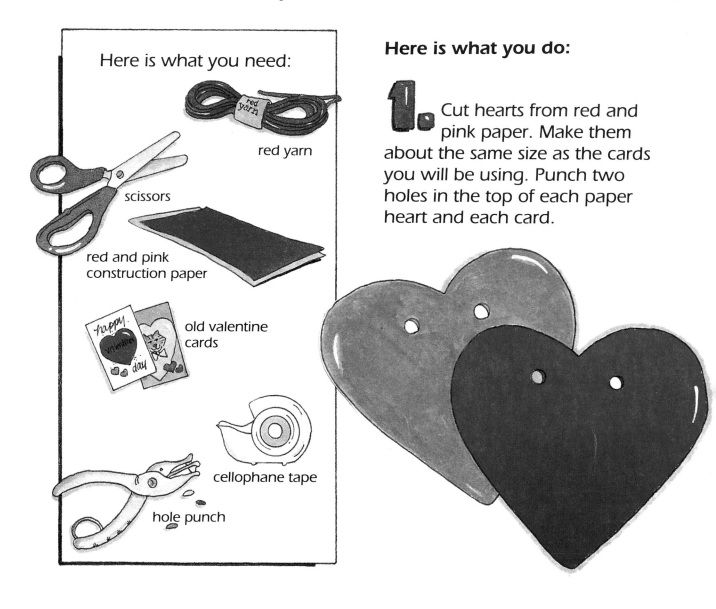

red yarn

scissors

red and pink construction paper

old valentine cards

cellophane tape

hole punch

Here is what you do:

1. Cut hearts from red and pink paper. Make them about the same size as the cards you will be using. Punch two holes in the top of each paper heart and each card.

2. Cut a length of red yarn as long as you would like your garland to be. String paper hearts and cards on the yarn, alternating hearts and cards and leaving about 1 inch (2.5 centimeters) between each one. Tape the yarn to the back of the hearts and cards to keep them in place.

This garland looks especially nice hung across a window. Use tape to hold the two ends in place.

TEACHER, Happy Valentine's Day! From Kathy

TEACHER YOU'RE A REAL TREAT!

Heart Man

Make this giant heart to keep you company this February.

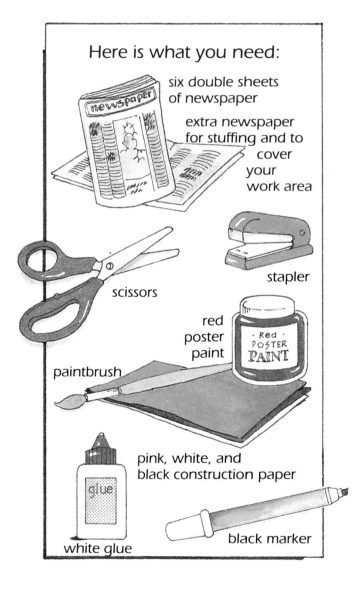

Here is what you need:

six double sheets of newspaper

extra newspaper for stuffing and to cover your work area

scissors

stapler

paintbrush

red poster paint

white glue

pink, white, and black construction paper

black marker

Here is what you do:

1. Fold six double sheets of newspaper in half. Use a black marker to sketch the outline of half a heart on the paper, placing the center of the heart on the fold and making it as large as possible. Leave the papers folded, and cut around the half heart outline.

32

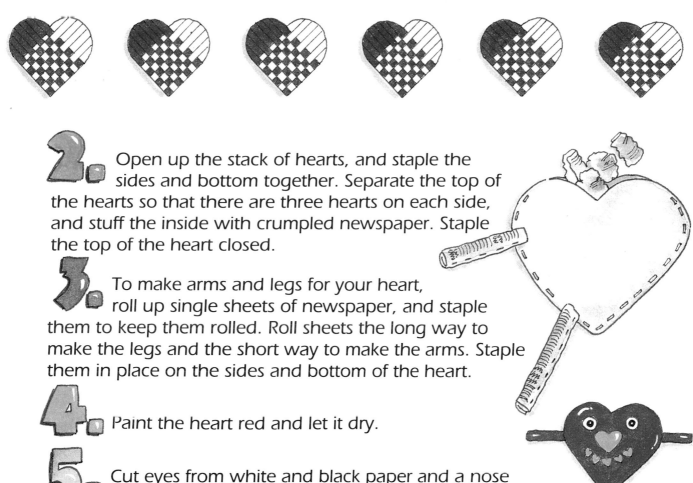

2. Open up the stack of hearts, and staple the sides and bottom together. Separate the top of the hearts so that there are three hearts on each side, and stuff the inside with crumpled newspaper. Staple the top of the heart closed.

3. To make arms and legs for your heart, roll up single sheets of newspaper, and staple them to keep them rolled. Roll sheets the long way to make the legs and the short way to make the arms. Staple them in place on the sides and bottom of the heart.

4. Paint the heart red and let it dry.

5. Cut eyes from white and black paper and a nose and mouth from pink paper. Glue them in place.

This cheerful fellow will need a chair of his own.

Valentine Picture Easel

This picture easel is like giving a little bit of yourself for a valentine. I bet you know someone who would like that!

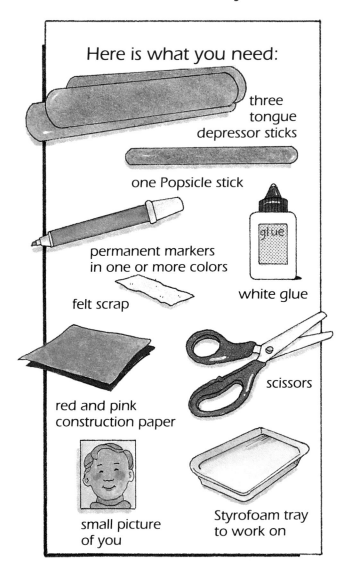

Here is what you need:

three tongue depressor sticks

one Popsicle stick

permanent markers in one or more colors

white glue

felt scrap

scissors

red and pink construction paper

small picture of you

Styrofoam tray to work on

Here is what you do:

1. Color all the sticks on both sides with permanent markers.

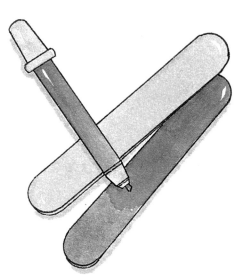

2. Glue the ends of two tongue depressor sticks together to form an upside down V.

Glue the Popsicle stick across the middle to form a ledge. Let the glue dry.

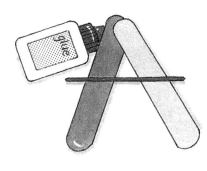

3. Cut a small hinge of felt. Glue one end to the top back of the two joined sticks, and glue the other end to the end of the last stick. Let the glue dry. The easel will now stand up if you carefully balance the back stick.

felt

4. Cut a square of red paper to fit on the front of the easel. Cut a pink heart to fit on the red square and glue it in place. Glue your picture in the middle of the heart. Glue the red square to the front of the easel.

This would look very nice on your Dad's desk.

Hanger Heart Sachets

What smells so pretty?

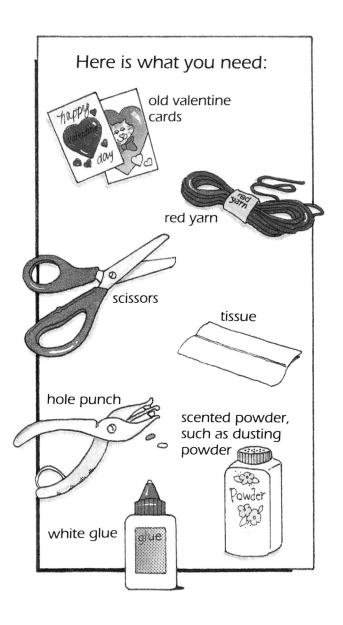

Here is what you need:

old valentine cards

red yarn

scissors

tissue

hole punch

scented powder, such as dusting powder

white glue

Here is what you do:

1. Cut two identical hearts from two cards.

2. Glue the sides and bottom of the hearts together with the pictures on the outside. Let the glue dry.

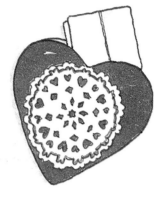

3. Wrap some powder in a tissue, and tuck it inside the pocket formed by the two hearts.

4. Punch a hole through the tops of the hearts, and string a piece of red yarn through the holes. Tie the yarn to pull the tops of the two hearts together. Then tie the ends of the yarn together to form a loop to hang the heart sachet from.

Hang a heart sachet on a hanger in your closet to make your clothes smell very nice. Heart sachets also make great gifts.

Valentine Guest Soaps

Here is what you need:

soap flakes

water

red food coloring

measuring cup

mixing bowl and spoon

pink plastic wrap

heart- and flower-shaped cookie cutters

pretty stickers

pink yarn

Here is what you do:

1. Put two cups of soap flakes into a mixing bowl. Squeeze a few drops of red food coloring into 1/4 cup of water, and add it to the soap flakes. Mix until the soap is evenly colored. If the mixture sticks to your fingers, add a little more soap. If it is too dry and crumbly, add just a tiny bit more water.

2. Press small amounts of the mixture on a clean counter, and cut heart and flower shapes with the cookie cutters. Put the shapes on a plate, and let them dry and harden for two days.

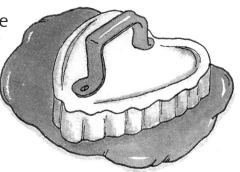

3. Decorate each soap with a pretty sticker. Wrap three or four soaps in a square of pink plastic wrap, and tie with pink yarn.

If you don't have any stickers to decorate your guest soaps, use little pictures of hearts and flowers cut from old greeting cards. Just attach them with a tiny dot of white glue.

Heart Magnets

Here is what you need:

two wooden ice cream spoons

scissors

white glue

red nail polish

nail polish

alphabet macaroni

self-stick magnetic strip

Here is what you do:

1. Cut 1 inch (2.5 centimeters) off the wide end of each spoon for a big heart and 1 inch off the handle end of each spoon to make a small heart.

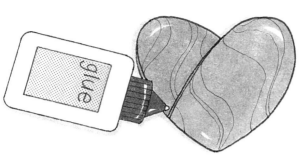

2. Place the pieces across each other and glue in place to form the hearts.

3. When the hearts have dried, glue a piece of magnetic strip on the back of each heart. Paint both hearts with red nail polish, and let them dry again.

If you would like to write a name or message on your hearts you can do this by gluing on tiny macaroni letters.

I LOVE YOU

Heart Photo Locket

Make your Mom a surprise locket.
The surprise is a picture of you!

Here is what you need:

two pry-off bottle caps

red and pink felt scraps

red nail polish

red yarn

a picture of your face small enough to fit inside a bottle cap

white glue

scissors

Styrofoam tray to work on

Here is what you do:

1. Paint both sides of both bottle caps with red nail polish. Let the polish dry completely before continuing.

2. Cut a small strip of red felt. Glue one end inside each cap to form a hinge that will allow the caps to close to form a locket.

3. Glue a circle of red felt inside one cap and a picture of you, cut to fit, inside the other cap. Close the locket and glue a tiny heart cut from pink felt to the outside.

4. When the glue has dried, tie a piece of red yarn around the hinge of the locket. Then tie the two ends together to form a necklace.

When someone asks your Mom who made her pretty necklace, she can open it up and show them.

Valentine Scrapbook

Make a special scrapbook to keep your valentines in. It is fun to look back the next year and find favorite old cards from favorite old friends.

Here is what you need:

four brown grocery bags

newspaper

red tissue or wrapping paper

matching ribbon

white glue

old greeting cards

scissors

Here is what you do:

1. Cut each of the bags along the seam. Then cut the bottom out so that you have four long pieces of brown paper. Stack the four pieces and fold them in the middle to form a book.

2. Make a heart pattern from newspaper to exactly fit over the front of the book. Then trim the book into the shape of a heart. Be very careful to leave a part of the folded side of the book uncut so that it holds together.

3. Use the newspaper pattern to cut a pretty cover for the book from wrapping paper. Glue the wrapping paper heart to the front of your book.

4. String ribbon through the center of the scrapbook and tie the ends in a bow at the front of the book. Cut the letters of your name from old greeting cards and glue them on the front of the book.

Fill your book with pretty valentines.

File Folder Letter Keeper

This pocket file is just right for *saving special letters and cards.*

Here is what you need:

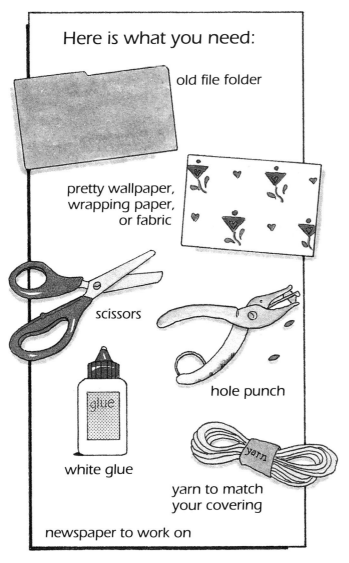

old file folder

pretty wallpaper,
wrapping paper,
or fabric

scissors

hole punch

white glue

yarn to match
your covering

newspaper to work on

Here is what you do:

1. If the folder has a tab on one side, trim the tab off to make the edge even. Lay the file folder open on your work surface, with the outside surface up. Cover the entire outside with glue.

Cover the folder with pretty paper or fabric and trim to fit.

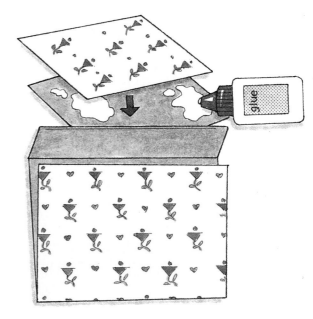

2. While the glue is still wet, fold the folder like an envelope with a flap. Let it dry folded.

3. Punch holes along both sides of the folder and lace the sides together with yarn. Punch a hole in the center of the edge of the flap. String a long piece of yarn through this hole and tie it. Use the yarn to tie the folder shut.

What a great place to stash a love letter!

About the author and illustrator

Twenty years as a teacher and director of nursery school programs have given Kathy Ross extensive experience in guiding young children through craft projects. Her craft projects have appeared in **Highlights** magazine, and she has also written numerous songs for young children. She lives in Oneida, New York.

Sharon Lane Holm won awards for her work in advertising design before shifting her concentration to children's books. Her illustrations have since added zest to books for both the trade and educational markets. She lives in New Fairfield, Connecticut.